ALL ABOUT ME

Name

Email

School

Grade

Address

Room

Phone

School Year

USERNAMES & PASSWORDS

RESOURCES

STUDENTS

NAME	PARENT/GUARDIAN	ADDRESS

PHONE/EMAIL

NOTES

HAPPY BIRTHDAY!

JULY

AUGUST

SEPTEMBER

OCTOBER

NOVEMBER

DECEMBER

CELEBRATE!

JANUARY

FEBRUARY

MARCH

APRIL

MAY

JUNE

HOLiDAYS &

JULY

4 Independence Day

› Park and Recreation Month

AUGUST

9 Book Lovers Day

› Get Ready for Kindergarten Month

SEPTEMBER

11 Patriot Day

› Labor Day (1st Monday)

› Grandparents' Day (Sunday After Labor Day)

› Hispanic Heritage Month (Sept. 15–Oct. 15)

› Rosh Hashanah (or October)

› Yom Kippur (or October)

› Native American Day (4th Friday)

OCTOBER

24 United Nations Day

31 Halloween

› Columbus Day (2nd Monday)

› Fire Prevention Week (2nd Week)

NOVEMBER

1 National Family Literacy Day

11 Veterans Day

13 World Kindness Day

› Thanksgiving Day (4th Thursday)

› Hanukkah (or December)

DECEMBER

25 Christmas Day

26 Kwanzaa Begins

31 New Year's Eve

SPECIAL DATES

JANUARY

1 New Year's Day

> Martin Luther King, Jr. Day (3rd Monday)

> Chinese New Year (or February)

FEBRUARY

2 Groundhog Day

14 Valentine's Day

> Black History Month

> Presidents' Day (3rd Monday)

MARCH

17 St. Patrick's Day

> Women's History Month

> Easter (or April)

> Passover (or April)

APRIL

1 April Fool's Day

22 Earth Day

> National Poetry Month

MAY

1 May Day

5 Cinco de Mayo

> Asian-Pacific American Heritage Month

> Teacher Appreciation Week (1st Week)

> Mother's Day (2nd Sunday)

> Memorial Day (Last Monday)

JUNE

14 Flag Day

> Pet Appreciation Week (1st Full Week)

> Father's Day (3rd Sunday)

> National Safety Month

WEEKLY SCHEDULE

TIME	MONDAY	TUESDAY	WEDNESDAY	THURSDAY	FRIDAY

Considerate
FRiENDLY loving
TENDER Helpful
WARM
big-hearted DEAR
KiND CARiNG
GOOD
GENEROUS MAGNANIMOUS
AFFABLE

JULY

SUNDAY	MONDAY	TUESDAY	WEDNESDAY

THURSDAY	FRIDAY	SATURDAY

Notes

_____
_____
_____
_____
_____
_____
_____
_____
_____
_____
_____
_____
_____
_____
_____
_____
_____
_____
_____
_____
_____
_____
_____
_____
_____
_____
_____
_____
_____

Notes

"Be kind whenever possible. It is always possible." —Dalai Lama

Books to Read:

AUGUST

SUNDAY	MONDAY	TUESDAY	WEDNESDAY

THURSDAY	FRIDAY	SATURDAY

Notes

Great way to go! MARVELOUS!

I'm proud of you

YOU MAKE ME SMILE

SUPER DUPER

AMAZING EFFORT

Outstanding Performance

Keep at it

KEEP UP THE GOOD WORK

I'M IMPRESSED

Bravo!

You've Made Progress

WRITE COMPLIMENT CARDS TO SEND HOME TO EACH STUDENT

TRY TO ALWAYS FIND THE BEST in EACH of THEM

SEPTEMBER

SUNDAY	MONDAY	TUESDAY	WEDNESDAY

THURSDAY	FRIDAY	SATURDAY

Notes

Notes

Kindness T-Shirt Day

OCTOBER

SUNDAY	MONDAY	TUESDAY	WEDNESDAY

THURSDAY	FRIDAY	SATURDAY

Notes

"Always be a little kinder than necessary." —James M. Barrie

NOVEMBER

SUNDAY	MONDAY	TUESDAY	WEDNESDAY

THURSDAY	FRIDAY	SATURDAY

Notes

"A single act of kindness throws out roots in all directions, and the roots spring up and make new trees." —Amelia Earhart

DECEMBER

SUNDAY	MONDAY	TUESDAY	WEDNESDAY

THURSDAY	FRIDAY	SATURDAY

Notes

"Kindness in words creates confidence. Kindness in thinking creates profoundness. Kindness in giving creates love." —Lao Tzu

JANUARY

SUNDAY	MONDAY	TUESDAY	WEDNESDAY

THURSDAY	FRIDAY	SATURDAY

Notes

Class Activity

KiND VALENTINES

PARi GAVE ME A PENCiL.

* IRA * TAUGHT ME ROCK, PAPER, SCiSSORS. *

Malik gave me a High five.

Sara told me a funny JOKE.

MAYA HELPED ME iN MATH GROUP.

FEBRUARY

SUNDAY	MONDAY	TUESDAY	WEDNESDAY

THURSDAY	FRIDAY	SATURDAY

Notes

Notes

BULLETIN BOARD:
Lucky Clovers

I'm **Lucky** because I love my DOG.

I'M LUCKY BECAUSE MY BEST FRIEND LIVES NEXT DOOR.

I'm lucky because my teacher is nice.

I'm lucky because I get to PLAY BASEBALL.

I'M LUCKY BECAUSE MY LITTLE BROTHER LOOKS UP TO ME.

MARCH

SUNDAY	MONDAY	TUESDAY	WEDNESDAY
1	2	3	4
8	9 Science - 100% pp. 1+2 HW China Timeline 100% SSR ⇒ 40min	10 China Timeline 100% Science pp. 3+4 98% Science p.5 100% SSR ⇒ 45min.	11
15 CORONAVIRUS Pandemic	16 NO SCHOOL	17 NO SCHOOL	18 8:15 - 12:30 Math Test 100%
22	23	24	25
29	30	31	

THURSDAY	FRIDAY	SATURDAY
5 China Timeline in-class 100% #1+2 Math 1A 100%	6 China Timeline in-class 100% #3-9 Spelling Math 1B 100%	7
12 Math Test 97%	13 NO SCHOOL	14
19	20 NO SCHOOL (Feed the Homeless)	21
26	27 NO SCHOOL	28

Notes

Notes

"You cannot do a kindness too soon, for you never know how soon it will be too late." —Ralph Waldo Emerson

SHOWER of ⭐

COMPLIMENTS

CHOOSE A STUDENT
EACH DAY TO BE
SHOWERED with
COMPLIMENTS by
HIS or HER CLASSMATES

APRIL

SUNDAY	MONDAY	TUESDAY	WEDNESDAY

THURSDAY	FRIDAY	SATURDAY

Notes

Notes

"A kind word is like a spring day." —Proverb

Write
Thank You
Notes to
Building
Staff,
INCLUDING
CUSTODIANS, AND
CAFETERIA AND
BUS STAFF!

MAY

SUNDAY	MONDAY	TUESDAY	WEDNESDAY

THURSDAY	FRIDAY	SATURDAY

Notes

Notes

"Be a rainbow in someone else's cloud." —Maya Angelou

BE Kind TO Yourself.

CELEBRATE THE END of a Successful Year!

JUNE

SUNDAY	MONDAY	TUESDAY	WEDNESDAY

THURSDAY	FRIDAY	SATURDAY

Notes

Notes

NOTE to SELF:

You'll NEVER Regret Being Kind

Week #

Time: 8:15-8:45 Subject: Bible	Time: 8:45 - 9:45 Subject: History	Time: 9:45 - 10:55 Subject: Lang. Arts
MONDAY 3/9		
• Prayer • Personal Bible Lesson • Combined Bible • Memory Verse • Worship		
TUESDAY 3/10		
• Prayer • Student Bible • Combined Bible • Memory Verse • Worship		
WEDNESDAY 3/11		
• Prayer • Student Bible • Combined Bible • Memory Verse • Worship		
THURSDAY 3/12		
• Prayer • Student Bible • Combined Bible • Memory Verse		
FRIDAY /		

Time: 10:15 —
Subject: 11:15
Yoga : Lunch

Time: 11:15
Subject: 12:15
SSR

Time: 12:15 —
Subject: 2:15

Time: 2:15 —
Subject: 3:30

Week #

Time:	Time:	Time:
Subject:	Subject:	Subject:

MONDAY

/

TUESDAY

/

WEDNESDAY

/

THURSDAY

/

FRIDAY

/

Time:	Time:	Time:	Time:
Subject:	Subject:	Subject:	Subject:

Week #

Time:	Time:	Time:
Subject:	Subject:	Subject:

MONDAY

/

TUESDAY

/

WEDNESDAY

/

THURSDAY

/

FRIDAY

/

Time:

Subject:

Time:

Subject:

Time:

Subject:

Time:

Subject:

Week #

Time:	Time:	Time:
Subject:	Subject:	Subject:

MONDAY

TUESDAY

WEDNESDAY

THURSDAY

FRIDAY

| Time: | Time: | Time: | Time: |
| Subject: | Subject: | Subject: | Subject: |

Week #

Time:	Time:	Time:
Subject:	Subject:	Subject:

MONDAY

TUESDAY

WEDNESDAY

THURSDAY

FRIDAY

Time:	Time:	Time:	Time:
Subject:	Subject:	Subject:	Subject:

Week #

Time:	Time:	Time:
Subject:	Subject:	Subject:

MONDAY

TUESDAY

WEDNESDAY

THURSDAY

FRIDAY

Time:	Time:	Time:	Time:
Subject:	Subject:	Subject:	Subject:

Week #

Time:	Time:	Time:
Subject:	Subject:	Subject:

MONDAY

/

TUESDAY

/

WEDNESDAY

/

THURSDAY

/

FRIDAY

/

Time:	Time:	Time:	Time:
Subject:	Subject:	Subject:	Subject:

Week #

Time: Subject:	Time: Subject:	Time: Subject:

MONDAY

/

TUESDAY

/

WEDNESDAY

/

THURSDAY

/

FRIDAY

/

Time:	Time:	Time:	Time:
Subject:	Subject:	Subject:	Subject:

Week #

Time:	Time:	Time:
Subject:	Subject:	Subject:

MONDAY

/

TUESDAY

/

WEDNESDAY

/

THURSDAY

/

FRIDAY

/

Time:	Time:	Time:	Time:
Subject:	Subject:	Subject:	Subject:

Week #

Time:

Subject:

Time:

Subject:

Time:

Subject:

MONDAY

/

TUESDAY

/

WEDNESDAY

/

THURSDAY

/

FRIDAY

/

Time:	Time:	Time:	Time:
Subject:	Subject:	Subject:	Subject:

Week #

Time:	Time:	Time:
Subject:	Subject:	Subject:

MONDAY

/

TUESDAY

/

WEDNESDAY

/

THURSDAY

/

FRIDAY

/

Time:	Time:	Time:	Time:
Subject:	Subject:	Subject:	Subject:

Week #

Time:	Time:	Time:
Subject:	Subject:	Subject:

MONDAY

/

TUESDAY

/

WEDNESDAY

/

THURSDAY

/

FRIDAY

/

Time:	Time:	Time:	Time:
Subject:	Subject:	Subject:	Subject:

Week #

| Time: | Time: | Time: |
| Subject: | Subject: | Subject: |

MONDAY

/

TUESDAY

/

WEDNESDAY

/

THURSDAY

/

FRIDAY

/

Time:

Subject:

Time:

Subject:

Time:

Subject:

Time:

Subject:

Week #

Time:	Time:	Time:
Subject:	Subject:	Subject:

MONDAY

TUESDAY

WEDNESDAY

THURSDAY

FRIDAY

| Time: | Time: | Time: | Time: |
| Subject: | Subject: | Subject: | Subject: |

Week #

Time:	Time:	Time:
Subject:	Subject:	Subject:

MONDAY

/

TUESDAY

/

WEDNESDAY

/

THURSDAY

/

FRIDAY

/

Time:	Time:	Time:	Time:
Subject:	Subject:	Subject:	Subject:

Week #

Time: Subject:	Time: Subject:	Time: Subject:

MONDAY

/

TUESDAY

/

WEDNESDAY

/

THURSDAY

/

FRIDAY

/

Time:	Time:	Time:	Time:
Subject:	Subject:	Subject:	Subject:

Week #

Time:

Subject:

Time:

Subject:

Time:

Subject:

MONDAY

/

TUESDAY

/

WEDNESDAY

/

THURSDAY

/

FRIDAY

/

Time:	Time:	Time:	Time:
Subject:	Subject:	Subject:	Subject:

Week #

Time:

Subject:

Time:

Subject:

Time:

Subject:

MONDAY

/

TUESDAY

/

WEDNESDAY

/

THURSDAY

/

FRIDAY

/

Time:	Time:	Time:	Time:
Subject:	Subject:	Subject:	Subject:

Week #

Time:	Time:	Time:
Subject:	Subject:	Subject:

MONDAY

/

TUESDAY

/

WEDNESDAY

/

THURSDAY

/

FRIDAY

/

Time:	Time:	Time:	Time:
Subject:	Subject:	Subject:	Subject:

Week #

	Time: Subject:	Time: Subject:	Time: Subject:
MONDAY /			
TUESDAY /			
WEDNESDAY /			
THURSDAY /			
FRIDAY /			

Time:	Time:	Time:	Time:
Subject:	Subject:	Subject:	Subject:

Week #

Time:	Time:	Time:
Subject:	Subject:	Subject:

MONDAY

/

TUESDAY

/

WEDNESDAY

/

THURSDAY

/

FRIDAY

/

Time:	Time:	Time:	Time:
Subject:	Subject:	Subject:	Subject:

Week #

Time:	Time:	Time:
Subject:	Subject:	Subject:

MONDAY

TUESDAY

WEDNESDAY

THURSDAY

FRIDAY

Time:	Time:	Time:	Time:
Subject:	Subject:	Subject:	Subject:

Week #

Time:	Time:	Time:
Subject:	Subject:	Subject:

MONDAY

/

TUESDAY

/

WEDNESDAY

/

THURSDAY

/

FRIDAY

/

Time:	Time:	Time:	Time:
Subject:	Subject:	Subject:	Subject:

Week #

Time:	Time:	Time:
Subject:	Subject:	Subject:

MONDAY

/

TUESDAY

/

WEDNESDAY

/

THURSDAY

/

FRIDAY

/

Time:	Time:	Time:	Time:
Subject:	Subject:	Subject:	Subject:

Week #

Time: Subject:	Time: Subject:	Time: Subject:

MONDAY

/

TUESDAY

/

WEDNESDAY

/

THURSDAY

/

FRIDAY

/

Time:	Time:	Time:	Time:
Subject:	Subject:	Subject:	Subject:

Week #

	Time:	Time:	Time:
	Subject:	Subject:	Subject:

MONDAY

/

TUESDAY

/

WEDNESDAY

/

THURSDAY

/

FRIDAY

/

Time: | Time: | Time: | Time:

Subject: | Subject: | Subject: | Subject:

Week #

Time:	Time:	Time:
Subject:	Subject:	Subject:

MONDAY

/

TUESDAY

/

WEDNESDAY

/

THURSDAY

/

FRIDAY

/

Time:

Subject:

Time:

Subject:

Time:

Subject:

Time:

Subject:

Week #

Time:	Time:	Time:
Subject:	Subject:	Subject:

MONDAY

/

TUESDAY

/

WEDNESDAY

/

THURSDAY

/

FRIDAY

/

Time:	Time:	Time:	Time:
Subject:	Subject:	Subject:	Subject:

....
....
....
....
....
....

....
....
....
....
....
....

....
....
....
....
....
....

....
....
....
....
....
....

....
....
....
....
....

Week #

Time:	Time:	Time:
Subject:	Subject:	Subject:

MONDAY

/

TUESDAY

/

WEDNESDAY

/

THURSDAY

/

FRIDAY

/

Time:	Time:	Time:	Time:
Subject:	Subject:	Subject:	Subject:

Week #

	Time:	Time:	Time:
	Subject:	Subject:	Subject:

MONDAY

/

TUESDAY

/

WEDNESDAY

/

THURSDAY

/

FRIDAY

/

Time:	Time:	Time:	Time:
Subject:	Subject:	Subject:	Subject:

Week #

Time:

Subject:

Time:

Subject:

Time:

Subject:

MONDAY

TUESDAY

WEDNESDAY

THURSDAY

FRIDAY

Time:	Time:	Time:	Time:
Subject:	Subject:	Subject:	Subject:

Week #

Time:

Subject:

Time:

Subject:

Time:

Subject:

MONDAY

/

TUESDAY

/

WEDNESDAY

/

THURSDAY

/

FRIDAY

/

Time:	Time:	Time:	Time:
Subject:	Subject:	Subject:	Subject:

....
....
....
....
....
....

....
....
....
....
....
....

....
....
....
....
....
....

....
....
....
....
....

....
....
....
....
....

Week #

Time:

Subject:

Time:

Subject:

Time:

Subject:

MONDAY

/

TUESDAY

/

WEDNESDAY

/

THURSDAY

/

FRIDAY

/

Time:	Time:	Time:	Time:
Subject:	Subject:	Subject:	Subject:

Week #

Time:	Time:	Time:
Subject:	Subject:	Subject:

MONDAY

/

TUESDAY

/

WEDNESDAY

/

THURSDAY

/

FRIDAY

/

Time:	Time:	Time:	Time:
Subject:	Subject:	Subject:	Subject:

Week #

Time:	Time:	Time:
Subject:	Subject:	Subject:

MONDAY

TUESDAY

WEDNESDAY

THURSDAY

FRIDAY

Time:	Time:	Time:	Time:
Subject:	Subject:	Subject:	Subject:

Week #

Time:	Time:	Time:
Subject:	Subject:	Subject:

MONDAY

/

TUESDAY

/

WEDNESDAY

/

THURSDAY

/

FRIDAY

/

Time:	Time:	Time:	Time:
Subject:	Subject:	Subject:	Subject:

Week #

	Time:	Time:	Time:
	Subject:	Subject:	Subject:

MONDAY

/

TUESDAY

/

WEDNESDAY

/

THURSDAY

/

FRIDAY

/

Time:	Time:	Time:	Time:
Subject:	Subject:	Subject:	Subject:

Week #

Time:	Time:	Time:
Subject:	Subject:	Subject:

MONDAY

/

TUESDAY

/

WEDNESDAY

/

THURSDAY

/

FRIDAY

/

Time:	Time:	Time:	Time:
Subject:	Subject:	Subject:	Subject:

Week #

	Time:	Time:	Time:
	Subject:	Subject:	Subject:

MONDAY

/

TUESDAY

/

WEDNESDAY

/

THURSDAY

/

FRIDAY

/

Time:	Time:	Time:	Time:
Subject:	Subject:	Subject:	Subject:

Week #

	Time:	Time:	Time:
	Subject:	Subject:	Subject:

MONDAY

/

TUESDAY

/

WEDNESDAY

/

THURSDAY

/

FRIDAY

/

Time:	Time:	Time:	Time:
Subject:	Subject:	Subject:	Subject:

Week #

Time:	Time:	Time:
Subject:	Subject:	Subject:

MONDAY

/

TUESDAY

/

WEDNESDAY

/

THURSDAY

/

FRIDAY

/

Time:

Subject:

Time:

Subject:

Time:

Subject:

Time:

Subject:

Notes

Design by Mina Chen. Illustrations by Joel Holland.